THE MIDNIGHT SOUP

Leo Burtin

2014–16

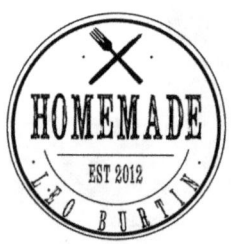

ISBN: 978-1-326-82849-3

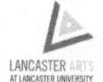
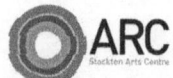

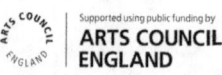

THE MIDNIGHT SOUP

Leo Burtin was born and grew up in the northeast of France. He initially trained with Transversales – Théâtre de Verdun and went on to read Theatre Studies at Lancaster University's Institute for the Contemporary Arts. In 2012, he began working on a series of artworks collectively titled *Homemade.*

Homemade seeks to interact with, explore and question the links between food, domesticity and (auto)biography. The project aims to playfully and poetically disrupt familiar and domestic contexts in order to create structures and contexts within which to have conversations, notably on value, identity, ageing, memory, death & dying and the concept of choice.

For I have known them all already, known them all;
Have known the evenings, mornings, afternoons,
I have measured out my life with coffee spoons;
I know the voices dying with a dying fall
Beneath the music from a farther room.
So how should I presume?

T.S. Elliott
The Love-Song of J. Alfred Prufrock

A group of people who have just met are exchanging
names. They are not exchanging names so that they
can identify each other. They are each giving away the
name they came in with, and choosing to accept
another.

Rajni Shah

Pour la Mamie Josette

FOREWORD

The Midnight Soup sometimes is a live performance for up to fourteen guests at a time. Each time it is presented, together with the audience, we prepare a meal for us to share at the end.

The performance follows a rigorous structure, in which I loosely navigate a number of roles.

Host, Storyteller, Cook, Guide, Listener, Stranger, Friend

...

The Midnight Soup sometimes is a humble, yet filling dish. Each time it is prepared, the ingredients change slightly, and it tastes a little different as a result.

The preparation of the dish follows a loose structure, in which you rigorously undertake a number of tasks...

Peeling, Chopping, Boiling, Grinding, Mixing, Stirring

...

The Midnight Soup sometimes is a way for me to invite you to have a conversation about a collection of complex thoughts I have had. Each time this conversation happens, the outcome is unpredictable.

The conversation follows a loose structure, in which I commit myself to rigorously listening.

The Midnight Soup sometimes is a book. Each time you read it, you may find something different.

The book follows a rigorous structure, in which we will rigorously, or perhaps loosely, engage with a number of ideas.

Memory, Family, Measuring, Death, Inviting

...

The Midnight Soup, in all of its forms, always begins with an invitation. Here, I invite you to think of this object as a collection of short stories, or poems... or better still, as a recipe book or a journal. You may dip in and out of it. You may skim read. You may cross some words out and make some notes, it's yours.

I may borrow the words of a favourite author of mine, Christophe Spielberger to also ask you to 'throw your old eyes away', and this is of course, merely an invitation. The choice remains yours.

The Midnight Soup, in all its forms, always ends with a celebration. Here, I will take the opportunity to celebrate the people who have contributed to its making, and the journey it has been to get to this point, to this object in your hands. It would be dishonest to not say that I will relish the chance to invite others to celebrate and respond to The Midnight Soup also.

The Midnight Soup, in all its forms, is a conversation starter.

It is about remembering, an it is about moving forward. It is about not knowing, it is about asking and it is about respect. It could be made by anyone and it is always for sharing. It is for keeping warm and it is for getting together.

Leo Burtin, London, November 2015

AN INVITATION

Bristol, 29th March 2015
Lancaster, 28th May 2015
Leeds, 19th July 2015
Stockton-on-Tees, 14th October 2015
Pudsey, 16th October 2015
London, 30th October 2015
London, 31st October 2015
Birmingham, 23rd January 2016
Margate, 29th January 2016
Sheffield, 16th April 2016
Lancaster, 6th May 2016
Sale, 19th May 2016

Dear Stranger, Dear Friend,

You are invited.
To supper and to a conversation.

In a moment, I will open the doors to

The Milk Bar
The Nuffield Theatre
The Den
The Studio Theatre
The Community Hall
The Theatre
The Fin Bar
The Meeting House
The Auditorium
The Chambers

...

Together, we will gather to make and eat The Midnight Soup. Together, we gather to listen to a story, and to share our own.

The Midnight Soup starts as a monologue, and in gentle and unpresuming ways opens out to become a conversation. It tells the story, of an unremarkable woman, who every day, sat down to meticulously record the facts of her life in a diary, until one early summer day, she chose to end her own life.

The Midnight Soup is the love letter of a grandson to his grandmother, it is also an edible memorial, celebrating a life lived to the rhythm of the seasons.

It is about losing someone you love, to themselves. It is about remembering, and it is about moving forward. It is about not knowing, it is about asking and it is about respect.

The Midnight Soup could be made by anyone and it is always for sharing. It is for keeping warm, and it is for getting together.

It is possible that some of you may find parts of this conversation upsetting. If you need to take a break from the conversation and leave the space for a while, feel free to do so. You will be welcome to take your seat again at any time.

The Midnight Soup is suitable for vegetarians and vegans, and the show does not contain any nuts. If you have any allergies or dietary requirements we should be aware of, please let your usher know now.

You may also take this opportunity to wash your hands. Before we begin, I would like to thank you for being here today.

...and I hope that you will be able to stay for a while afterwards to celebrate the community of people who have once called the Milk Bar home... Whether for a short hideaway, or for several years...

...And it seems wise to let you know that today marks the first ever public performances of *The Midnight Soup*...

...and it seems appropriate to let you know that I began making *The Midnight Soup* right here in Stockton and that I am especially pleased to be presenting the show here...

It feels important that you chose to take the time to be here for this conversation in bustling London...

Sharing this with you on the eve of All Saint's Day seems appropriate, after all...

...It has been ten years since my grandmother began writing the diary which inspired this performance. I have been wanting to tell you about her for just as many...

...Here in Margate is as close as I'll get to her village during this tour...

...It's been almost a year since I showed a first version of the piece here in Lancaster. It's good to be home...

...It's been just over a year since I put the final touches to the text of the show, not far from here, looking out to Salford Quays...

Warmest wishes,
Leo Burtin

GATHERING

I have been pacing in the space, retreated behind closed doors until you have all arrived. I want you to be welcomed as a group, to start with. I want us to walk into the space together, as one unit. I don't tell you this, but at this point, I am hoping we might become a *community*, for the next few hours. I am aware of the fact that it is a complicated word, *community*. I am aware that this could fail, and that I have no way of being sure what a it being success might look like anyway.

I take a deep breath, and I come and find you.

Most of the time, you don't notice me at first, so I take a moment to look at you, to hear you, to feel what might be going on, right here, right now.

I take a deep breath, and I greet you.

> Hello, my name is Leo Burtin, and I will be your host for this evening's performance of *The Midnight Soup*. How are you?

Sometimes you don't answer straight away, sometimes you don't answer at all. Sometimes it's okay, and sometimes I worry that you already don't like me. Then I don't let myself worry about it too much and I continue.

In just a moment, I will lead you into the theatre. As you come in, you will see a long table, with chairs around it. In front of each chair, there is a name. Find yours, and take a seat.

I come in last, unless I'm holding the door for you. I might help you find your name, and gesture to a space where you can leave your coat or your bag. I might help you find your place. You might tell me I've spelt your name wrong, or that your friend isn't coming anymore. It's all fine, we settle together. I sit last.

I take a deep breath and I look at you.

> Thank you for being here.
> Thank you for responding to the invitation that you received, whichever form it might have taken.

I ask you to turn your placeholder around, so I can see your name.

> It's important to me that we can call each other by our first names.

Sometimes, not always, I will show that behind the card on which my name is written, I keep another piece of paper.

Sometimes, not always, I will read it out to you.

> *A group of people who have just met are exchanging names. They are not exchanging names so that they can identify each other. They are each giving away the name they came in with, and choosing to accept (**one**) another.*

Sometimes, not always, I accidentally add the word *one* as I read, and it works beautifully too.

> In the invitation that you received, there was a gentle warning. Some of the conversations we will have this evening, some of you might find a little upsetting. If this is the case, and you wish to take some time away, please do so.

You will be welcome to take your seat back at any point.

While we are focused on each other and that it is easy to forget the world beyond, I simply want to signal that the space is always open. That you always have a choice. You may stay, or you may go. You may change your mind.

> This evening we will be preparing a meal together, for us to share at the end. We will be having conversations while we do so. To start with, I will do most of the talking and at various points, I'll invite you to speak, if you'd like to.

In the background, gently, quietly, almost imperceptibly, the radio is playing. A clue to the world outside. A gentle, mechanical distraction. Just in case you need it, just in case I want it.

I tell you I'd like to ask you some questions.

ASKING

What is your understanding of where you are at, right now, in your life?

What do you want to achieve most?

What is your greatest fear?

What would be unacceptable to you?

You can write at your own pace, take your time. You needn't think too much. You can be reassured your answers won't be read out loud. You won't need to do anything else with them.

You know there will be one more question, but that you won't be answering it for a while.

Sometimes, not always, I might ask you another question or two. You don't need to write this time. I would like you to speak your answer. I simply want to invite your voice into the space, for you to see what it feels like.

REMEMBERING

Today, I would like to tell you about my grandmother.

JOSETTE BURTIN née LAHAYE
1934–2012

I would like to tell you about who my grandmother was in the year 2006.

It is the year I have the most facts about – here they all are, written neatly, almost religiously. Next to details about the local economy, the T.V. programme and occasionally, history.

I would like to talk about the fact my grandmother chose her own death. She picked the date, the time, the place and the means.

I don't know the facts of how well prepared she was or how many times she had thought it might be the day.

Until recently, I had chosen not to remember what day it was.

I would much rather remember, being here today

I would much rather remember...

14th December

3rd October 1995 with Hilary
1st April with Jason

24th April 2008 with Sarah

5th March 2006 with Daniel

7th September 2003 with Ali

12th March 2013 with Danny

13th September 2009 with Marcus

25th April with James

27th October 1989, 24th July 2003, 30th September 1990 with
Stella

23rd March 1984 with William

12th September 2015 with Emily

13th October 2005, 1st May 1997, 16th October 2009
with Ruth

2nd February 2001 with Jon

24th September 1993 with Ashleigh

7th August 2010 with Saffy

3rd June 2012 with Alex

30th January 2014 with Josh

13th January 2013 with Ruth

6th December 2007 with Julia

20th May 2008 with Jen

11th January 1994

11th January 2004

23rd April,

7th May,
8th May, with Deborah

19th December 2013 with Sarah

19th December 1975,
6th December 1959,
12th September 1955,
24th May 1928,
Saturday 4th March 2006 with Emma

22nd February 1989 with Nina

I would much rather remember, being here today

FOLLOWING

1. You may eat as much bread as you like at any point, but you'll have to make sure you still have plenty of room for the main course when it's ready.

2. You may not place your elbows on the table.

3. When drinking, your nose cannot be inside the glass.

4. You may talk amongst yourselves, but not with your mouth full.

5. You may not talk while the head of the table is addressing the family.

6. Please do not slurp or make your teeth grind against the cutlery.

7. You will have to finish your dinner. Ideally, you will even use bread to mop up. If you really can't manage, please let the head of the table know as soon as possible so permission not to finish your food can be assessed and granted.

8. If you leave any food, you will not be allowed any dessert.

Someone once turned a rule which said
NO DANCING AT THE TABLE
into the promise that
there will be dancing at the table.
And there was, and it was delightful.

BEGINNING, AGAIN & AGAIN

This evening, I would like to tell you about someone you've never met.

I have a few facts: here they all are, written neatly, almost religiously, next to details about the local economy, the T.V. programme and occasionally history.

I could start like this:

Wednesday 21st February 1934.

In rural northern France, Josette Lahaye is born. The event is modestly celebrated, and it is not long before life goes back to what is normal, there and then.

Some 5 years later, a war breaks out.
We are on the borderline, we are on the frontline.

The previous war is too close for us to have much hope that it will pass. We are grateful that out here, in the countryside, we have all that we need. Or perhaps this is the way we like to remember it.

There is going to school, there is going to church, walks in the woods, looking for mushrooms and flowers on the first of May... There is hard graft and joyous traditions. There is always gratefulness.

Le silence est d'or, la parole est d'argent.

Then I'd like to think you fall in love. That you meet him, Jean Burtin, at the ball. I'd like to imagine that it's 14th July, Bastille Day, that you've both had a few glasses of wine, and that he asks you if you'd like to dance, in a thick, Lorrain accent which makes you giggle.

I'd like to think that at that point, you make a choice you'll continue to believe in for years to come.

Fast forward, and two boys are born.

I'll imagine that life isn't all that different, that you just get on, that it's all a natural progression.

There are no major events, until Jean dies.
The boys are teenagers, and they are tough, so you're not alone.

You won't ever be.

Your son, my uncle, will be right next to you until the end. You'll see your other son regularly, and he'll call almost every week. At least one of your grandchildren will be there for each of the school holidays.

I could start with an anecdote.

> *Aserejé ja deje tejebe tude jebere sebiunouba majabi an de bugui an de buididipí*
>
> *Aserejé ja deje tejebe tude jebere sebiunouba majabi an de bugui an de buididipí*
>
> Las Ketchup

I could start by telling you that research shows that elderly people are more likely to complete suicide than any other age group worldwide.

I could start by telling you the Ancient Greeks gave elderly people the option of assisted suicide if they could plead convincingly that they had no useful role in society.

I could start with memories.

There's standing on a chair to reach the top shelf of the kitchen cupboard, lifting a heavy dictionary, and spending the afternoon reading its pink pages.

There's picking cherries to make conserves with, one for me, one for you, one for the pan, one for me, one for you, one for the pan.

There's shelling peas, sat on a wicker chair, by the old chicken house.

There's juicing oranges and leaving the peels to dry on the radiators, to get rid of kitchen smells.

There's chocolate shavings on buttered bread, on Wednesday afternoons, to eat while watching cartoons together.

There's the day we read about *pain azyme*.

We read about where it came from, we look the word up in the dictionary, we find out that it comes from the Greek.

Unleavened.

We become present to its biblical origins.

It is the bread that travels through time, space and cultures.

Together, and without a time-machine, we become time-travelling explorers, we become historians and linguists, we become storytellers and chefs.

Together, we fold the water into the flour, a sprinkling of locally mined salt, far from the deep sea, sea salt that the Ancient Romans, the early Jews would have used.

Together we invent, we interpret, we experiment and try again.

Together, we eagerly await the arrival of our guests, so they may try it, so we may share it, so we may break it.

Together we rehearse the story of our day, so that when together, we sit at the table, we too will have something to share.

Together, from the kitchen and without a time-machine we now know that we are time-travelling explorers, historians and linguists, storytellers and chefs.

I could start with a weather report.

WEATHERING

To wear away or change the appearance or texture of (something) by long exposure to the atmosphere

(Of rock or other material) be worn away or altered by long exposure to the atmosphere

(Of a ship) come safely through (a storm)

Withstand (a difficulty or danger)

12th March
It has iced over, it's white. The sky is blue from early morning, but clouds start to appear later on.

23rd March
Grey sky, it is windy, it gets brighter, the sun attempts to come out.

29th March
The sky is grey with occasional bright breaks in the clouds. It is getting slightly colder.

1st April
Grey skies and torrential rain.

24th April
From the morning, the sun is white as they say, it's already very cloudy, but it's nice out.

24th July
Heat wave, very very hot.

7th September
In the morning, a few clouds, during the day, it is nice and warm, there is a light breeze.

13th September
Another beautiful day.

27th October
Grey morning, with a little rain. Superb afternoon.

21ˢᵗ FEBRUARY 1934

It is a Wednesday.
It is sunny and exceptionally dry.

In cinemas, Claudette Colbert and Clark Gable are Ellie Andrews and Peter Warne in Frank Capra's *It happened one night*. In Quebec, the Legislative Assembly refuses to pass women's suffrage.

276,000 babies are born that day.

There is one other date which I remember.
78 years, 3 months and 10 days later. 30ᵗʰ May 2012. It is a Wednesday. On the day she dies:

Hindu devotees take a holy dip during the Ganga Dussehra festival.
Workers unload a lorry full of humanitarian aid for Nuban refugees.
German president Joachim Gauck visits Israel and the Palestinian territories.
Serena Williams is defeated by Virginie Razzano during the French Open.
Queen Elizabeth II holds a Garden Party at Buckingham Palace.
Former Liberian President Charles Taylor is sentenced to 50 years in prison.

It is the feast day of Joan of Arc, commemorating the anniversary of her death.

2006

It starts with melting snow, and family visits are in order for season's greetings. There's well wishes, brioches and yule logs. There's bubbles from the champagne going straight to your head. There's annual phone calls to old friends, and preparing responses to New Year's cards, with your neat handwriting.

There's the children going back to school, and you put another white wash on. The weather warms up, and you iron. The weather warms up and you mop.

The nights are getting darker, the nights follow day, quicker, it seems.

There's the weekly shopping list and thinking about what to make for lunch, and for dinner.
There's noticing the rain coming and going.
There's going to the hairdresser's and making a note of presidential speeches.
There's visits from friends and making pancakes for dinner.

There's treating yourself to takeaway pizza.
There's phone calls from your son.

There's celebrations.

There's a note that on 10th January 2006 62,900,000 people live in France.

There's anecdotes about celebrities you hear about on the radio.

There's sharing a bench with a neighbour.

There's cleaning the house, methodically.
There's reading magazines.

There's paying bills, and a little bit of DIY.
There's baking, together or alone.
There's buying baguettes from Peggy the Baker.

There's looking words up in the dictionary, and writing them down.
There's being invited to a birthday party, and politely declining.
There's going for a walk.

There's noting you might have written something twice.

You're happy that we don't forget your birthday, and you never forget ours.

There's commemorating an earthquake that took place three years ago.

It's a Winter Olympics year, and you mark the last day, at the top of the page.

There's looking after the garden.

There's collecting things, for little or no reason.

There's making sure we go with the leftovers.

There's making a note of the birds you see, and of course, the changes in the weather, always.

This kind of diary, of journal, in French, is called *journal intime*.

There is of course something profoundly intimate about this document. There is only ever one voice, one that, if you had ever met Josette Burtin, you would be able to recognise, you would be able to hear in the writing.

You would be able to translate the neatness of the handwriting into a distinctly Lorraine accent attempting to be cleaner, to be less flat, to be more clever.

You would see a lively, curious, active woman behind the accumulation of banal knowledge, the classification of facts, the making of lists, the weather reporting, the phone call recording, the bookkeeping.

There is also a lot of intimacy missing.

Tuesday 5th December 2006

"Their father would have been 73 today"

Nothing more than a hint, a sense that she remembered. A sense that it was one of the dates that mattered to her.

This journal, along with over 60 other diaries could have been written by anyone.

There are many unknowns, many empty spaces, many pauses. There are a few facts, a few memories, a few inconsistencies.

It is a record of banal histories.

I'd like you to imagine any of your elderly relatives.

I'd like you to celebrate their banal histories, the epic web of their stories. The feelings, the misunderstandings and the unspoken love the simple word family conjures.

The word family comes from the Latin.

Famulus.

Famulus stands for servant.

I was surprised by a sense of oppression when I first found that out.

I soon left it behind to remember a sense of duty.

Duty of care.
A sense of loyalty.

I'd like you to think of those who *serve* in your family.

It is with pain that we are announcing the brutal death of Josette Burtin née Lahaye, which occurred 30th May 2012.

Mrs Burtin was 78 years old. The religious ceremony will take place on Tuesday 5th June, at 10 a.m., following which, according to her will, she will be cremated.

No flowers, no wreaths, no commemorative plaques.

30th May 2012

Aujourd'hui j'annule tout mes rendez-vous

Today, I cancel all my appointments.

She didn't write that it was the day before the earliest sunrise this month, or that it was almost unbearably hot.

She didn't write that the radio talked about Hindu Devotees, Nuban Refugees, Presidents, past and current, a defeat at tennis, and a garden party.

She didn't make a note at the top of the page that it is the feast day of Joan of Arc.
"

> The stories told to make sense of suicide must be respected. They signify attempts to inject clarity into a social phenomenon that is always far from clear.
> The suicide note, for example, sometimes functions as a written attempt to seek such clarity – if not for its writer, then for those who read it. It may have been written, or be read, as an act of contrition, or as a purchase ticket for forgiveness and closure – a kind of moral token of exchange in the narrative economy of

life and death. The suicide note is an artefact of social history for local historians, belonging to everybody and nobody simultaneously. Although meeting with an often reluctant reception, it functions as a social symbol, in part about closure – a final testimony – and as a story that is continually up for grabs as to both its real meaning and moral significance."

Alec Grant,
*Exploring the idea of a rational basis
for suicide and its social implications*, 2015

I do not have her final testimony, her last diary.
Only 2006.

It is the year I have the most facts about – here they all are, written neatly, almost religiously. Next to details about the local economy, the T.V. programme and occasionally, history.

This is also artefact of social history for local historians, belonging to everybody and nobody simultaneously. It may have been written, or be read, as an act of contrition, or as a purchase ticket for forgiveness and closure.

It may have been written, or be read, as an act of remembrance,or as a celebration of the changes in the weather and shared meals.

Together, and without a time-machine, we become time-travelling explorers, we become historians and linguists, we become storytellers and chefs.

In my family, I think the cooking is most definitely northeastern.

I grew up in Lorraine.
Ich komme aus Lothringen.

Lorraine isn't, and doesn't feel as German as the neighbouring region; Alsace.

Through both wars, shifting borders, and later 'pendulum commuting', things have slowly, gently seeped through the cracks...

Like Chinese whispers, we make our own version of things...

The Midnight Soup is a Chinese whisper.
Mitternachtsuppe.

Historically, Mitternachtsuppe, was served part way through nights of heavy drinking, during the all night balls of the festive season.

It was a way of lining your stomach, absorbing the alcohol... It's a rich soup; packed with proteins and carbs.

It is for keeping warm and it is for getting together.

The Midnight Soup has whispered its way from a fancy ball dish to something you put together from the leftovers in your fridge, combined with the staple eastern European spice; paprika and chopped tomatoes. The Midnight Soup is a Chinese whisper.

Mitternachtsuppe. Le Bouillon de Minuit.

We all make choices, all the time.

We make them, because we make them. Whether we've considered them at length, or made them on the spot. We make them and keep going.

All that happened is that she made choices.
She picked the date, the time, the place and the means. I don't know the facts of how well prepared she was, or how many times she had thought it might be the day.

What is your understanding of where you are at, right now, your life?
I'm dying, very slowly.

What do you want to achieve most?
To be remembered.

What is your greatest fear?
Being the last person on Earth.

What would be unacceptable to you?
Not having a choice.

I know she had said it a few times.

"I will know when it's time, and I will drink the Midnight Soup."

She too had Chinese whispered her Midnight Soup. She put together and mixed up her German *Mitternachtsuppe* and her French *bouillon de onze heures* – the eleventh hour broth, the last supper.

I have questions I can no longer ask. I have feelings that can't be helped – of sadness, and of anger.

I have choices that I make. I chose to invite you, and I chose to have this conversation. I will listen, intently to all that you have to say. I will answer, authentically, all of the questions you can still ask.

I stand for choice, and it is my choice.
Nothing more, nothing less.

The Midnight Soup is a conversation starter.

It is about remembering, and it is about moving forward.

It is about not knowing it is about asking, and it is about respect.

The Midnight Soup could be made by anyone and it is always
for sharing.

It is for keeping warm and it is for getting together

ASKING

Is there anything you are thinking about now, that you weren't thinking about before?

IT HAPPENED ONE NIGHT
Emma Geraghty

So if I write everything down, I won't forget. I'll try not to trip over my words, I will try to give you an honest account of this night. It's worth remembering.

The theatre is not a theatre, not tonight.

We go through the same doors into the darkness, but onto the stage. Under the lights. We take off our coats, drop our bags, and set ourselves. Our names are already there. The table has been expecting us, and who knows how long it has been waiting.

distribuer des assiettes / planches a découper / couteaux tranchants / vous servir de l'eau

There is a story. A story of a life lived with the passing of the seasons on their eternal cycle, a story faithfully inscribed on page after page after page of diaries. Time is marked differently here.

visites de sa famille / fleurs du jardin / deux baguettes de Peggy / cadeaux pour la fête des mères

There are rules for this performance, as there are rules for everything to do with performing. But the rules are not rules for the theatre, not tonight. The rules are family rules, handed down through time. You must finish everything on your plate, and if you don't there will be no dessert. Don't talk when the head of the table is talking. No elbows on the table.

We talk while we work, timeless in our tasks. Chopping oignons, l'ail, les poivrons, les courgettes, les champignons. Everything for the pot, making more food than the eight of us need, because more food is always better. We can have a second helping, we can save it for the next night, we can share it with others.

And there is a story, a story of a life lived for every individual day, a story that is magical in the mundanity of every individual day.

Le théâtre n'est pas un théâtre, pas ce soir. Or any other night. With these rules and actions and stories comes the simple elegance of the dinner party. Because that's what it is – *un dîner*, a space to share. We sit and we talk about everything and everyone, finding out as much as we can about each other without being too intrusive, exchanging stories for memories for anecdotes. As if we know that, when we leave the table, we won't be seeing each other again. There will be no catch up phone calls. No coffee dates. No dropping round unannounced because you forget your hat. It will all be gone. So we share the stories along with the food and the wine and rejoice in the moment. It brings us together as strangers with so many unrealised similarities. And to say we leave as friends would be clichéd, but we do leave as something more than what we were when we first sat down.

And with this dinner party, with its rules and actions and stories and elegance, come several questions. One stands out. What would be unacceptable?

Ce qui serait inacceptable?

De ne pas avoir le choix.

Not having a choice.

The idea of suicide in any presentation is provocative. It triggers people. And at the beginning, the advice is given that this is a safe space, that some of the things you hear may make you feel uncomfortable or upset, if you want to leave the table for a bit and then come back then that would be fine. We're given a choice.

So let it be known that Josette Burtin, being sound of mind, body and soul, took her own life. And let it be known it was her choice. Because it can be. It's something to do with free will, with the freedom of choice that simply being human grants us. It's something to do with a life lived from season to season, an acknowledgement that time upon this earth is finite, and why the hell shouldn't we get to choose when and how and where we go? And let it be known that I hope to one day feel that completion, to have that courage, because we're not afraid of dying, we're afraid of forgetting, of our mind and body and soul splitting off from each other and not leaving directions. Let it be known that I, too, am afraid of forgetting.

Si je vous écris tout, je ne vais pas oublier. Je n'oublierai pas. Je vais essayer de ne pas trébucher sur mes mots, je vais essayer de dire la vérité. On se souvient.

We make a choice. We raise a glass. To life. To tonight. To the dates we hold dear, the days we'd rather forget, and the nights we choose to remember. To time travellers. To chefs.

Pour Josette

RECIPE FOR A MIDNIGHT SOUP

It starts with an invitation
It starts with being grateful
It starts with getting to know each other, a little
It starts with a gentle warning
We ask that you all make the first mark
We ask you: what do you want?
We tell you a few facts we know

> *and at this point it starts with onions, and garlic quickly follows*

We ask for your advice
We lay the rules

> *and at this point, we ask you to share your own rules, and we take care of the things that may need to cook for a while longer...*

We tell you about someone you've never met
We tell you about the negative space, the pauses, and the gaps.
We tell you what we know and we do not know.

> *and at this point we take stock, we stir and add, we spice up and check*

We paint a portrait: short, neutral, dry and cold, to start with.
We tell you an anecdote
We give you a context; background information
We tell you about learning together, we teach you something
We go back to the beginning: we tell you about the weather
We paint a portrait; warm and inaccurate
We invite you to imagine it could be about anyone

We remember who served and we share

We skip to the end.

> *and at this point, we put in the final ingredients, the things that don't need to cook for very long, we stir, smell and adjust.*

We fill in the gaps, the empty spaces, the pauses.
We reveal the game of Chinese whispers.

We ask you simple questions; we invite you to make choices.
We answer complex questions, and we state standing for something.

We prepare to serve, we promise to listen intently and to communicate authentically.

We serve, and we share.

We be together

ASKING

Can you describe what the weather is like?

Can you tell me something interesting about today?

Can you tell me about a connection you made with somebody today?

Can you tell me about one of your meals?

Can you share a thought with me that you've not shared with anyone else yet today?

Can you tell me something about your future?

RECIPE FOR A MIDNIGHT SOUP

Many people have asked me to share the recipe for the soup we prepare during the show, my interpretation of a Midnight Soup... This is my attempt at providing some kind of guidelines for making it... Do improvise around it though, taste as you go, and adjust... I won't give any proportions... Make it with what you've got, for however many people you have to feed. Make sure you have some leftovers... it's always nicer the next day.

Firstly, gently fry a mixture of diced red and white onions in a generous helping of olive oil, in a large saucepan. As the onions start to soften and brown, add a generous portion of finely chopped garlic.

Then add any vegetables that will benefit from being fried off and that you wish to use... Peppers, courgettes, mushrooms are all an excellent choice.

Add a generous helping of both smoked and sweet paprika (about half and half), a little bit of salt, and a hearty portion of freshly cracked black pepper. Stir well to coat your vegetables in the spices and seasoning. Reduce the heat and let the vegetables gently cook.

Meanwhile, prepare a stock of your choice. I usually use a vegetable cube with some tomato puree. Make enough to cover your vegetables. Before adding the stock to the pan, add dried thyme to your vegetable mix.
Add the stock, and let the mixture boil for a while. Once it has reduced slightly, add tinned chopped tomatoes in their juice to thicken the stock.

Let it simmer before adding any vegetables that would benefit from being boiled (such as broccoli) and your choice of beans. I like to use chickpeas, red kidney and cannellini.

Cover and simmer until piping hot.

Serve with warm crusty bread and top with fresh thyme. Add hot sauce and seasoning to taste.

THANKING

The Midnight Soup was made with:

Mark Whitelaw
Dramaturge, Director, Collaborator
Becci Sharrock
Creative Producer
Aly Howe
Technical & Production Manager
Rajni Shah
Mentor
David McBride
Lighting Designer
Lucille Acevedo-Jones
Design Consultant
Adam York Gregory
Graphics & Web Design
Phil Cole
Assistant Producer

And with thanks to: Catherine Shaw, Ewa Witaszek, Andy Smith, Ali Matthews, Tim Jeeves, Alice Booth, Caroline MacLennan, Lindsay Bradshaw, Jamie Eastman and all the staff at Lancaster Arts, Annabel Turpin, Daniel Mitchelson and all the staff at ARC, Matthew Eames and all the staff at the Lowry Studio, Morag Iles and all the staff and residents at Space Six, Ella Good, Nicki Kent and all Residence members, all tour stops hosts & promoters. Michael Druce, Dipak Kanbi, Jatin Luthia, Edson Williams, Susann Ribeck and all at Landmark Worldwide. Emma Geraghty, Jenny Gaskell, Gareth Cutter, Zoe Mann, Lois Weaver, Lyn Gardner.

www.ingramcontent.com/pod-product-compliance
Lightning Source LLC
Chambersburg PA
CBHW072250170526
45158CB00003BA/1044